Shouting at the Ocean

Poems that make a SPLASH! A fantastic, hilarious and sometimes thoughtful collection of poems by some of the best poets writing for children in the UK today.

Shouting at the Ocean

Poems chosen by
Graham Denton, Andrea Shavick and Roger Stevens

Illustrations by
Cathy Benson, Liz Brownlee, Philip Waddell
and Sue Hardy-Dawson

Cover illustration by
David Parkins

Book design by
Stephanie Bartlett and Joe Decie

For Lily and Ruby, Bernie & JP
(may you never stop seeking new oceans to shout at)
and for Archie, the naughtiest cat in the world.

Hands Up Books
1 New Cottages
Spout Hill
Brantingham
East Yorkshire
HU15 1QW
handsup@handsup.karoo.co.uk

Poems © the authors (2009)
Illustrations © the illustrators (2009)
Cover © David Parkins (2009)
This collection © Hands Up Books (2009)

Illustrations by
Cathy Benson (pages 7, 29, 44, 46, 50, 80)
Liz Brownlee (pages 31, 32, 48, 63, 73)
Sue Hardy-Dawson (pages 19, 39, 65, 67)
Philip Waddell (pages 13, 22, 27, 36, 54, 77)

In the spring a group of children's poets
spent a week together writing poems, reading poems
and talking about poems. They went for walks, gazed at
clouds, built castles in the sand and generally behaved
like children. This is the book they wrote.
You can find out a bit more about them at the end.

Shouting at the Ocean

Gerard Benson

Last week the sea was whispering,
hushing and shushing the beach,
sifting its salty secrets into the sand.

But this evening the moon is full
and the sea's found its voice; it bellows and roars,
sings aloud, booms in the Smugglers' Cave.

And me? I'm shouting right back at it,
shouting at the ocean. Full-voiced.
I fill my lungs and let go.

I call out my name over and over,
then other words. Roller! Smash! Crash!
Wow! Boulder! Ocean! Ocean! Ocean!

The wind comes whistling and lifts my words
and carries them over the waves.
Wow! Roller! Ocean! Ocean! Ocean!

Hello Mum, I'm on the Bus

Roger Stevens

Hello, Mum.
Yes, I'm on the bus.
No, I'm fine.
I left my homework behind. Could you…
Yes, I know it was a silly thing to do.
So could you…
Yes, I am forgetful…
Yes, luckily it is screwed on.
Anyway, could you…
It's on my desk, next to…
I know I should have made my bed…
Yes, it is in a bit of a mess…
I know…
I was in a hurry because I overslept…
Yes, I should have gone to bed earlier
But I was doing my homework…
Anyway, about my homework…
Could you bring it to the…
Okay, I'll tidy my room tonight. Mum?
Could you…
We're here now. I've got to get off.
I'm at the school.
About my homework… don't bother.
I'll say the hamster ate it again.
Bye, Mum.

Reasons

Jan Dean

I didn't pass the test
Because they asked all the wrong questions.
They didn't ask a single one
About good stuff, or stuff that's fun.
They showed no interest at all
In TV, PCs or football.
They never even touched upon
The way to eat a sticky bun
Or how to talk to caterpillars
Or any stuff that really matters,
Like yo-yoing or pogo-sticking,
Climbing trees or lolly licking.
That test was seriously uncool,
They never asked a thing about important stuff
Only about the stuff we did in school…

TV Rap

Bernard Young

After school
what suits me
is to sit on the carpet
and watch TV.

Watch TV
Watch TV
I sit on the carpet
and watch TV.

I burst in
about half past three.
Kick off my shoes
and get comfy.

Get comfy
Get comfy
I kick off my shoes
and get comfy.

Dad says, 'You're too near.
Take my advice.
Move further back
or you'll damage your eyes.'

But my eyes don't hurt
and they haven't turned square.
Close to the screen
is what I prefer.

When I get home
what pleases me
is to sit on the carpet
and watch TV.

I watch TV
I watch TV
and I don't budge
until it's time for tea.

Time for tea
Time for tea
I don't budge
until it's time for tea.

Going to the Café with Grandad

John Rice

When I go to the café with Grandad,
he hangs his hat from a hook on the shelf.
I get that sweet 'n' lovely feeling
    that I've got him all to myself.

When I go to the café with Grandad,
    he orders a teacake and coffee.
He says, "Whatcha fancy on yer toast?
    Butter, jam or toffee?"

When I go to the café with Grandad
    he talks to Mrs MacPherson.
He tells her I'm his granddaughter
    and I'll soon be a famous person.

When I go to the café with Grandad
    I talk about teddies and toys.
He says he never had such things,
just played football with the boys.

When I go to the café with Grandad,
    he says, "Ach, it's a sad old life."
He talks a lot about Granny
    and that he misses his dear old wife.

When I leave the café with Grandad,
we step out into the rain.
He starts jumping around in puddles
sloshing water down the drain!

I love going to the café with Grandad,
for breakfast or afternoon tea.
But I like it best when it's busy,
because then I can sit on his knee.

Family Meals

Michaela Morgan

My gran bakes.
The oven glows warm and full
with pies and stews and cakes
that take their time.
Comfy, warm and slow,
smells drift and grow until
"Here you are, love."
The house is peaceful, warm and still.
My gran has the time.

My mum fries.
She fries and grills and boils.
Food sizzles and fizzes,
steams, spits and hisses
and splatters like a greasy firework.
Then clatter BANG! "It's done!
Hurry up! Must run!"
Behind her the door shuts with a crash.
My mum has to dash.

My dad shrugs.
His cupboard is bare.
"Everything I make goes up in smoke!"
He grins uneasily, tries to joke.
He buys me burgers – double cheese, large fries,
chocolate milkshake – giant size,
"Anything you want, O.K.?"
He ruffles my hair. "See you Sunday."
My dad goes away.

Bring and Buy

Rachel Rooney

Sold my mother at the Summer Fayre
to a Year 3 kid. Good buy.
Six quid. A bargain at half the price...
didn't think twice, I swear.
Found a great mum going spare:
big boots, spiked hair – dyed pink.
So walked her back to mine. Like mates,
our footsteps fell in synch.

Dined on take-aways, lay in bed
but fed-up quick with fast food,
mess and being late for Miss.
Took her away instead.
Swapped her for another mother.
This one smarter: slick
side-parting, high-heeled shoes, posh skirt.
Looked like an advert. Tricked.

Should have guessed the rest: the muesli,
manners, star charts, tests,
in bed by eight and no buts. Please,
she's got to leave. Can't wait.
Then met my real mum,
good as new and maybe better.
Told that kid in Year 3, when he's through
I'll pay out a tenner to get her.

A Bit of a Power Thing

Jan Dean

I am the Space-Time Continue Mum,
The cold blue universe rests in my hands.
I am the Space-Time Continue Mum,
I shrivel planets to burning sands.
When I speak stars shiver and quiver and quake,
When I roar suns blaze hotter then crumble and break.
All of the galaxies worship, revere me,
Nothing that lives doesn't bow down and fear me.
So crawl through the dust, do not dare to come near me!
For I am the mother of all mother stuff
The cosmos falls still when I shout, 'Enough!'
So, little one, little one, listen and hear me:
I am the Space-Time Continue Mum
And you will obey my decree,
So finish your homework this minute
And clean up your room before tea!

How to Successfully Persuade Your Parents to Give You More Pocket Money

Andrea Shavick

Ask, request, demand, suggest, cajole or charm
Ingratiate, suck up to, flatter, complement or smarm
Negotiate, debate, discuss, persuade, convince, explain
Or reason, justify, protest, object, dispute, complain
Propose, entreat, beseech, beg, plead, appeal, implore
Harass, go on about it, pester, whinge, whine, nag and bore
Annoy, insult, reproach, denounce, squeal, scream and shout
Go quiet, subdued, look worried, fret, brood, tremble,
shiver, pout
Act depressed, downhearted, upset, snivel, sigh
Go all glum and plaintive, wobble bottom lip and cry
Sniff, sulk, grumble, stare at ceiling, mope, pine, stay in bed
Get cross, get angry, fume, seethe, fester, agitate, see red
Provoke, enrage, push, bully, aggravate and goad
Screech, smoke, burn up, ignite, spark, detonate, EXPLODE

And if all that doesn't work

Here are two little tricks
That should do it with ease
No 1: smile
No 2: say please.

A Conversation with Uncle Ned

Gerard Benson

"I'm hot," said my uncle,
"Give me a pottle of bop."
"A pottle of bop?" I said.

"You know what I mean," Uncle said,
"A lottle of bemonade."
"How much is a lottle?" I asked.

"Son't be dilly," he said,
"You understand me werfectly pell –
A dizzy frink!"

"A dizzy frink," I said,
"Why can't you frink tap water
Like everybody else?"

"Wap tauter!? I need something
With bots of lubbles. Something
To nickel my toes," he cried.

But I'd stopped listening to him
And gone back to beading my rook.

Ig-pay Atin-lay

Rachel Rooney

Ig-pay Atin-lay is-hay ite-quay easy-hay
En-whay ou-yay earn-lay e-thay ules-ray.
I-hay ink-thay ey-thay ould-shay onsider-cay
eaching-tay it-hay in-hay ools-schay.

Pig Latin (Translation)
Pig Latin is quite easy
when you learn the rules.
I think they should consider
teaching it in schools.

Ten Books for Literacy Hour

Gerard Benson

Where are They Now?	by *Miles Aweigh*
Nothing to Eat	by *M.T.Tumms*
Don't Do That	by *Y.Knott*
I Know the Answer	by *R.U.Shaw*
How to be a Doctor	by *Ophelia Pulse*
I Know that Name	by *Isabel Ringing*
Snow on my Collar	by *Dan Drough*
How to Get Rich	by *Robin Banks*
I'm a Star!	by *Oscar Winner*
My Brother Played for England	by *Betty Diddant*

Tall Story

Sue Hardy-Dawson

A
tall
story
came
to our
house
today.
The
more I talked the more it grew. It

Bits   wouldn't
of   go
it   away
got
tangled
and
jammed
up all
the stairs
I didn't mean
to   start it
but it   didn't
seem to   care
I tried   very
hard to   hide it
underneath   my bed
but it just kept   getting bigger
with every   word I said
Eventually   because of it
some more   began to grow
They started   as excuses
that grew all   on their own.
So now I don't   know what to do
with such a   dreadful fibber
'cause every time   that I explain
it just keeps   getting bigger

I Am the Kid

Bernard Young

I am the kid who says 'Break's over'
at exactly 10.44.
I am the kid whose job it is
to knock on the staffroom door.

We haven't drunk our coffees yet!
I wish you'd go away!
That child is such a pest!
are the sort of things they say.

They're never pleased to see me.
How the insults fly!
But I don't care if they're put out.
I love to hear them sigh.

I am the kid who says 'Time's up.'
The kid they don't adore.
Because I am the kid whose job it is
to knock on the staffroom door.

(And I am the kid
who's looking forward
to upsetting them again
at precisely 1.04)

Revenge

Jan Dean

Just after I had painted Jake with honey
And staked him to the anthill in the yard,
A meteorite came hurtling from the heavens
And crashed down on the bike shed – which was hard
Because 6B were hiding out there
Trying to avoid the litter-pick
But now they are the litter – poor dear sweethearts.
Now that they're gone I don't feel quite so sick
Of all this teaching lark.
And if another class upsets me, well…
A small adjustment to the canteen custard –
A speck of cyanide will dispatch them to the dark.
Then I will walk the echoing corridors
A smile upon my face
Enjoying the quiet of the tidy classrooms
Where all is calm
And everything is in its proper place.

The First Doughnut

Roger Stevens

Miss Monty threw the first doughnut
(Miss Monty's a bit of a card!)
But it hit Mr Mooner
(who has no sense of humour)
and he threw it back – terribly hard.

Miss Monty ducked and it bounced off her chair
And hit Mr Jenkins' bald head.
He went ballistic
And threw back a biscuit
But it hit Mrs Thistle instead.

Soon the whole staffroom had joined in the fray
Throwing biscuits all over the place
Then in came the head
Mr Walton, who said… Yeugh!
As he caught a cream cake in the face.

"That's enough," barked the startled head teacher –
An annoyed Mr Walton is SCARY!
As you might suppose
Everyone froze
(He makes the Hulk look like a fairy).

"Who's to blame for this mess in the staffroom?"
"Pray tell me, who started the fight?"
Then from inside his jacket
He produced a big packet
Of chocolate marshmallows – he said, "RIGHT!"

Then with a lightning arm action
A flick of the wrist quite precise
With a maniacal laugh
He pelted the staff
And hit everyone at least twice.

"When you're having fun," he chuckled
"How quickly the time seems to pass
"So I'd just like to say
"I've enjoyed today's play
"There's the bell. Now get back to your class."

Ten Dinner Ladies

Andrea Shavick

Ten dinner ladies standing in a line
Until one realised it was the kids who were supposed to do that,
so then there were nine

Nine dinner ladies washing up the plates
Until one had an allergic reaction to the washing-up liquid,
so then there were eight

Eight dinner ladies scoffing cream teas in Devon
Until one had her GPS mobile tracked by the Head who sacked her for bunking off school,
so then there were seven

Seven dinner ladies dismantling the school by removing all the bricks
Until one happened to be inside the building when it collapsed,
so then there were six

Six dinner ladies chopping up onions and chives
Until one got such watery eyes she drowned,
so then there were five

Five dinner ladies shopping in the local store
Until one reached a little too far into the freezer and was
gobbled up by a frozen chicken,
so then there were four.

Four dinner ladies mopping up the kitchen with squeegees
Until one slipped on the wet floor and did an Olympic gold-
standard backflip into a pot of boiling beetroot,
so then there were three

Three dinner ladies lacing the rice pudding with glue
Until one stuck her fingers up her nose and couldn't breathe,
so then there were two

Two dinner ladies sunbathing in the playground under a red-
hot sun
Until one realised the other one had been burnt to a crisp,
so then there was one

One dinner lady entered a cooking competition, and won!
Now she's a famous TV cook and not a dinner lady anymore
– that's why there are none.

Watching

Andrea Shavick

What if I told you
The teachers in the staffroom
Were not really teachers at all
But vampires!
Flashing and gnashing their razor-sharp teeth
Spying on you
Watching your every move
Try and imagine it...
Now knock on the door
And ask for the Register
If you dare…

Hippo

Liz Brownlee

A hippo has skin that looks rubbery,
filled to bursting with all that is blubbery,
when his mouth opens wide
he could fit you inside,
thank goodness he only eats shrubbery!

Rumblies

Sue Hardy-Dawson

The Rumbly in your tumbly has a
rumbly tumbly voice. He will rumble,
mumble, grumble, till he gets his food of
choice. He'll gurgle out his verbals if you
won't be   his slave and
go raiding   in the kitchen
to try and   calm his rage.
Ravenous   he rails at you
stamping   on intestines.
Griping on   indefinitely
To threaten   indigestions.
His appetite's enormous. His desire to
be full. He resonates reverberates and
makes your senses dull. He punctuates
your puddings with little grunts for more.
He'll wake   you in the
Morning   with a
rumble   tumble
roar. He's   noisy
when it's   quiet
he loves   being
rude. He   doesn't
care who's   listening
because he wants more food. But giving
Rumblies all they ask is a mistake no
one must make. 'Cause if you over
feed them they just make your elly ache!

Granny's Teeth

Catherine Benson

When Granny's teeth were getting less,
she got some from the NHS.
She said, "They're grand. What can I bite?"
and sampled everything in sight.
But eating beef one day for lunch
they rapidly began to munch.
With eerie power they clicked and chewed,
mashing, mushing up her food.
Poor Granny cried, "I've had enough.
I know the steak was rather tough
but now I order you to halt!"
They took it with a pinch of salt,
and ever faster chomped the stew,
then turned on Gran and ate her too.

Snippets Of Sweeney Todd's Ingratiating Barbershop Chatter

Philip Waddell

A good afternoon Sir
And how do you do?
The weather is hot Sir
Yes, we're baking too.
You new around here Sir?
Oh, just passing through!

A very smart suit Sir –
Nice that shade of rust,
Makes you look a toff Sir,
Yes, real upper crust,
I don't flatter you Sir
No – take it on trust!

We're nearly done now Sir
Just finish you off.
Yes, sharp Sir – my razor,
So try not to cough!
Just my little joke Sir
We do like a laugh!

Some more off the top Sir
And then a blow dry?
Oh dear I slipped Sir –
So sorry – Oh my!
But still a neat cut Sir...
You'll look nice as pie!

Customers of Sweeney Todd, the demon barber of Fleet Street, were sometimes turned into fillings for meat pies!

Grandma was Eaten by a Shark

Andrea Shavick

Grandma was eaten by a shark
Dad, by a killer whale
And my baby brother got slurped up
By a rather hungry sea snail
A cuttlefish cut my mum to bits
An octopus strangled my sister
A jellyfish stung my auntie's toes
Giving her terrible blisters
A pufferfish poisoned my grandpa
A dogfish ate my cat
And then a catfish ate my dog!
I was very upset about that
So you go for a swim if you like
Just don't ask me to come too
I'm staying here with my camera
I can't wait to see what gets you!

Overheard on Safari

Gerard Benson

Look!
There's a flock of elephants
Galumphing across the horizon.

Herd of elephants.

Of course I've heard of elephants.
I was just telling you.
I saw a flock of them over there.

Herd!

Not from here you can't have.
Unless you've got sharper ears than mine.
You can't hear them from here,
Even a big flock like that.

It's a HERD of elephants!

Yes I know. Of course it is.
I've got eyes in my head.
I was just pointing them out to you.

The Piranhas in Guyana

Michaela Morgan

An iguana can alarm ya
It can give you quite a shock.
A crocodile won't make you smile
And a toad can give you spots.
Your granny's big fat budgie
Can give a nasty peck,
But the piranhas in Guyana will go straight for your neck.

The llamas in Lima will spit and stamp their feet.
A rhino looks ridiculous
And rarely smells too sweet.
The humble cod
Can be quite odd;
The barracuda, ruder.
But the piranhas in Guyana tend to EAT the odd intruder.

Ants in your pants will make you squirm and wriggle.
A scorpion in your sock is no cause for a giggle.
Stripy wasps and hornets really are a pest,
But the piranhas in Guyana are far worse than all the rest.

The wallabies are wannabees,
They wanna scream and shout.
The lounging lizard's not up to much – he's just a layabout.
An ass is – just an ass.
A mule HAS to be mulish,
But the piranhas in Guyana are particularly foolish.

A rather peevish parrot might peck you on the nose.
A somewhat careless elephant might tread upon your toes.
A snake might sneak around you and squeeze you
till you're flat,
But the piranhas in Guyana are even worse than that.

A crocodile upon the Nile
May devour a passing child.
The mildest hippopotamus may sometimes go quite wild.
The tiniest little tadpole could give a nasty . . . suck.
But meet one of these piranhas
And you're REALLY out of luck.

An Elephant is Born

Liz Brownlee

Night holds them safe,
the cloud moon gleams,
deep in the darkness
of soft breath and dreams,
the elephant mother
greets her new son,
with a tender and gentle
low, soft hum,
she strokes his face
the night-left long,
and sings her newborn
elephant song.

Easter Monday

Catherine Benson

We tied the white eggs in onion skins,
wrapped them round with string.
We boiled them for so long
the water looked like strong tea.
Lifted out, the string was dirty khaki,
but the eggs – the eggs were glorious
marbled brown, amber and yellow.
When we were at the top of the hill,
when the others rolled theirs down to crack,
I held mine back –
it was too beautiful.

Blake's Tyger - Revisited

Michaela Morgan

Tiger! Tiger! Turning white
In a cage just twice your height.
Six paces left, six paces right,
A long slow day, a longer night.

Tiger! Tiger! Dreaming still
Of the scent? The chase? The kill?
And now? No need. No place. No scope.
No space. No point. No hope.

Tiger! Tiger! Paces. Paces.
Once he flashed through open spaces.
His world once echoed to his roars.
Now he's quiet. He stares. He snores.

An inch of sky glimpsed through the bars.
A puddle. Concrete. Smells of cars.
He sniffs the air. He slumps. He sighs.
And stares and stares through jaundiced eyes.

On hearing that tigers in captivity can gradually
lose their colour, losing their camouflaging stripes
and fading slowly to white.

Pet Hates

Jane Clarke

Come on in. Don't mind Rex,
he's very tame, you'll see.
Sit down. Oh look! Rex likes you -
his head is on your knee.

Yes, I've worked hard to train him
since he hatched out of his egg.
Rex can fetch and walk to heel,
roll over, sit and beg.

He loves his tummy tickled,
he never goes out straying.
Well, yes, he bit my arm off,
but he was only playing.

He's licking you? He licks me, too!
Don't worry, Rex adores us.
You want to know what breed he is?
He's a Tyrannosaurus.

Don't run away, he'll think you're prey,
he can smell your fear.
Bad boy Rex! That's playing rough.
Down, Rex! Down! Oh dear...

A Dino-Store Dinosaur

Graham Denton

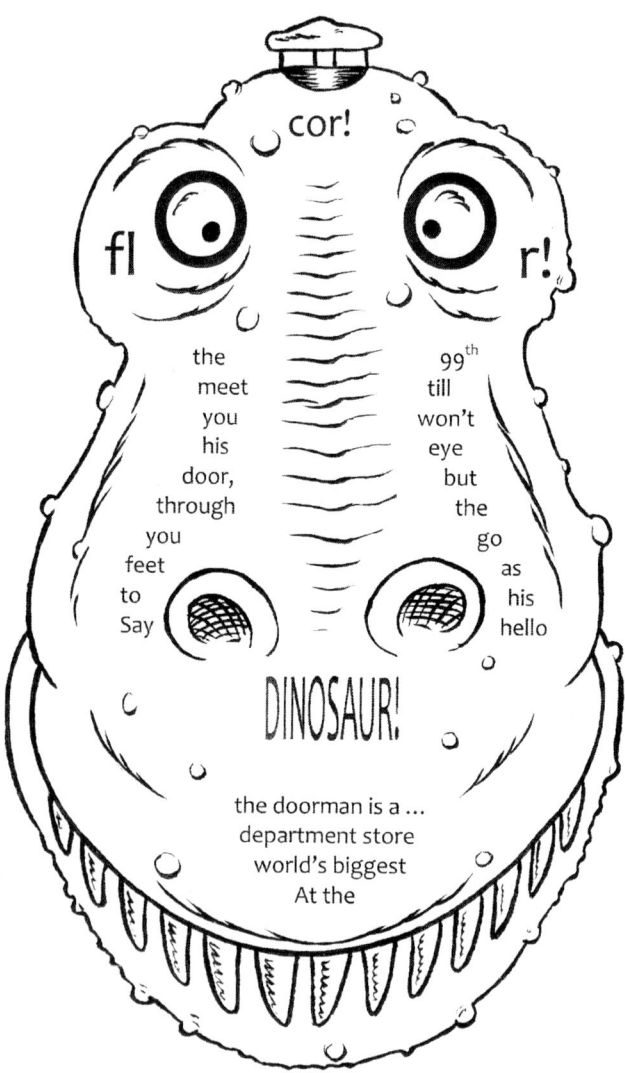

cor!

fl

r!

the 99th
meet till
you won't
his eye
door, but
through the
you go
feet as
to his
Say hello

DINOSAUR!

the doorman is a ...
department store
world's biggest
At the

Terrible Lizards

Sue Hardy-Dawson

Who says
There are no dinosaurs?
Hiding quieter than
mice under
fjords of
blue ice;
waiting
for the
land to
thaw;
dreaming
of their winter store
ancient dreams they've dreamt
before. Who says there are no dinosaurs?
Lurking darkly in deep pools; slumbering
inside green hills Enormous wings and dreadful
roar, burning eyes and horns that gore, trapped
beneath the ocean floor. Who says every dinosaur,
died of cold and turned to stone? Lumbering beast
with giant bones. Heavy feet and teeth that tore, deathly
grip and   iron jaw, armoured scales and fearful claw.
Who   says every last one died? Lurking darkly in deep
pools   Slumbering, inside green hills under   fjords
of   blue ice,   waiting   for the   world to
thaw   trapped   beneath   the   ocean
floor.   Who   says   every   last
one   died?   Perhaps   some   sleep
and
others
hide.

Kid in the City

Jan Dean

Kid in the city
stuck in the crowd
sees knees
and stone slab pavements,
kerbs and grids,
but mainly knees
coat hems and trainers
with chewing-gum stuck to the soles
thick threads trailing from denim jeans
frayed seams and shoes with buckles
that jangle like keys
but mainly knees.
Keep your head down -
no point in looking up
in this fat forest of people that could squish you dead
duck from the swing and bash
of shopping bags around your head.

Keep down in this swallowed up
swaying buzzing shuffle
where we are packed tight
as swarming bees,
where all a kid sees
is knees.
Oh please, spare me Saturday shopping
and knees KNEES KNEES.

The Sad, Sad Story of What Happened to the Three-Legged Dog That was Too Cheeky for His Own Good

John Rice

I went out for a jog
in the twisty-misty fog
    feeling super-duper fit and free.

Whilst running in the smog
I saw a three-legged dog
    and the three-legged dog saw me.

Then the three-legged dog
that was watching me jog
    cocked his back leg up against a tree.

I said "Hey, you naughty dog,
get away from that log!
    That's not where you should be!"

"Shut up you old tog,"
barked the three-legged dog
    "Go home and have a biscuit with your tea!"

"You cheeky little dog,
You've got manners like a hog,
       I'll teach you a thing or three!"

So I leapt fast as a frog
to catch the three-legged dog,
       he was slow as a sloth in a tree.

I caught the three-legged dog,
gave him a slip-slap-slog,
       now he's much more careful where he has a wee!

Ice Cream

Michaela Morgan

I dreamt of having a dog.
A racing dog.
A chasing dog.
An obedient amazing dog.

I got Scruff.
A rough dog.
A tough dog.
A run-in-circles-and-woof dog.

We were mates.
We liked the same things.
We liked running around the park.
We liked lying around the house.

And we liked eating,
especially ice cream.
We'd tried crisps
but they made him cough.

Shared sherbet made him foam.
Toffee stuck his teeth together.
Chocolate was one gulp then gone.
But ice cream...

He'd come running and smack his lips
then he'd be all laps and licks
and wags and shudders and shivers.
He became one huge wag of pleasure.
One excited quiver.

Sounds of bells on Saturday
announce the ice cream van.
Across the busy street I go,
 coins hot in my hand.

"Ice cream cornet please – with raspberry sauce."
Then Scruff comes running
and smack. Of course. A car
Hits him full speed on.

One startled yelp, one shudder and he's gone.
Not the slightest movement now.
Not the smallest sound.
Ice cream melting on to my foot.
Raspberry sauce sticky as blood.

Beastly Weather

Philip Waddell

After it's rained cats and dogs
They run off everywhere.
And when the land is white
It's deep in sleeping polar bear.
And when it's stinging hail
It's pelting hornets, wasps and bees.
And when we have thick mist these days
We can't see for the fleas!
And when it's bleak and humid
That's the earwigs and woodlice,
But when it's twinkling fireflies...
The evening's really nice.

At the Match

Liz Brownlee

They didn't like my earwig,
the reason I don't know…
But at the match they chanted,
earwig go, earwig go, earwig go...

The Bear in the Bin

Catherine Benson

The bear in the bin blinked his eye.
The bear in the bin was sad.
Tomorrow the dustman comes by.
The bear in the bin blinked his eye.
He had asked himself several times why
he'd been put in the bin. Was he bad?
The bear in the bin blinked his eye.
The bear in the bin was sad.

Poet-trees

Jane Clarke

Whenever life's unkind to me,
I run off to hug a tree.
I find it helps when I am sad
and stops me going barking mad.

If I'm downcast, depressed and blue
my only comfort then, is yew.
I do my weeping under willows
it saves on handkerchiefs and pillows.

Who needs regression therapy?
I'm back to my roots with a tree.
If seas of troubles overwhelm
I can step up and take the elm.

As I get alder, it's plane to see
my elders taught so much to me.
Now, when I'm fed up to the teeth
I just turn over a new leaf.

Someday, I may pine away,
but I try to keep my fears at bay
and rest on laurels when life's good –
and that is quite a lot... Touch wood.

Orang-Utan

Liz Brownlee

A heavy hulk and tum like mine
in shades of hairy clementine,
means when I'm up my forest tree
I live my whole life gingerly!

Miss Wise on Her Bike

Bernard Young

Fluorescent by day
Reflective by night
Miss Wise on her bike
Is a wonderful sight

She glides through the traffic
Freewheels past the jam
And all the time thinks
What a smart girl I am

I arrive on time
I don't pay to park
I'm soon at my desk
And ready to start

Then when my work's done
And it's time to go
I put on my helmet
My journey's not slow

When I take to the road
On the days I commute
I'm happy to say
I don't clog or pollute

Fluorescent by day
Reflective by night
Miss Wise on her bike
Is a wonderful sight

Double Rainbow

Catherine Benson

The sky
is violet
and indigo with rain.
The sun is low, a rainbow looks
amazed

at my
blue hat, green scarf,
yellow coat, orange gloves.
But most of all, it admires my
red boots.

When Fearsome Storm is Out to Plunder

Philip Waddell

When fearsome storm is out to plunder
And, round the landscape, wildly blunder;
When storm is out to rend asunder,
With flashing forks and hammer thunder...
Then find a place to shelter under
And pay respects in awe and wonder.

Balloonery Buffoonery!

John Rice

I hate balloons in packets,
red ones are the worst.
I hate them being blown up,
it scares me when they burst.

> *They're nastically plasticky,*
> *they're ballistically blasticky,*
> *they're drastically nasticky,*
> *they're bloodthirstically bombasticky!*

I hate balloons at parties
if they're in the hands of boys.
Or if the magician twists an animal
and there's that squeaky balloony noise.

> *It's excruciatingly nauseating,*
> *it's frustratingly abominating,*
> *it's gratingly penetrating,*
> *it's inflatingly aggravating!*

I hate balloons at Christmas
when they're dangling from the tree.
I shove my fingers in my ears,
in case they pop and scare me.

They're ponderously wonderous,
they're plunderously sunderous,
they're murderously blunderous,
they're gunpowderously thunderous!

(I'm the only balloonophobic in the
balloonophobicphonebook!)

What a Sucker!

Graham Denton

As a glassblower, Septimus Grayling
Had a rather regrettable failing.
When they laid him to rest,
He'd a PANE in his chest —
'stead of blowing, he kept on inhaling!

Just My Luck

Gerard Benson

The jailer turned his back,
It was time to try my flit,
So I made a bolt for the door,
But it didn't fit.

Post

Rachel Rooney

A queen in a palace, slumped on a throne
surrounded by servants but all alone.
Heavy with handshakes, bunches of flowers,
jewels, crowns, grinning for hours.
Fed up, bored, decided to quit.
So used her head and some royal spit.
Flicked through a book, picked a random address:
5, The High Street, Inverness.
Stuck her face on a card, destination beneath.
Does one fancy a swap, Ms Morag Mackeith?
Posted it off, didn't delay.
Saw herself landing, first class next day
with an inky tattoo (yesterday's date)
on a mat. Sat back. Couldn't wait.
That night she dreamt of burger and chips,
a part-time job with lunchtime kips,
allotment keys and charity shops,
queuing for loos, bingo, bus stops,
neighbours, backyards, The Christmas Club,
a seat by the fire in her local pub.
She tore up her diary, started to pack.
But Morag Mackeith never wrote back.

The Frog Princess

Sue Hardy-Dawson

Well
OK Dad, it was
something like this.   At
first I found him slimy   and
  I regret, wet. I know of course   looks aren't
    everything, I'm just not really sure   about green. So
      what if he did find my golden ball I didn't   once mention
        a kiss. More like I put him gently over the wall. Oh well
          then – maybe, as you suggest, it was the teeniest, little
            kick. Then naturally, I ran and ran as only really a true
              princess can, in silly shoes and a dress. I never once
                dreamed that he would follow – No. Dad   stop
                    don't   say a word imagine this he
                    wanted   to sleep on my pillow, to
              eat off the very   same plate. It really
              isn't   hygienic, a point
                                                   I tried but failed
                                                   to make. Well
                                                   at any rate, I
                                                  saw a flash
                                                and all at
                                                once, he was
                                                  such a dreamy date.
                                                    So we live in a pond,
                                                        where he is king,
                                                            the children
                                                                will hatch
                                                            in early spring,
                                                          yes it seems that
                                                    love changes
                                                everything.

Hopping Mad

Jane Clarke

I was happy as a froggy
in my smelly, stagnant pool.
I was one jump ahead.
I was free! Life was cool.
I got to move from pad to pad –
it really suits a bloke
to live a happy froggy life
until the day you croak.

I was happy as a froggy,
and the froggy life I miss,
ever since that stupid Princess
gave my froggy lips a kiss.
I'm a handsome Prince now,
but it doesn't make me glad –
I was happy as a froggy,
so it makes me hopping mad!

Love is Blind

Bernard Young

Under the mistletoe
my very short-sighted sister
and her extremely short-sighted boyfriend
take off their glasses
to kiss…
and miss.

Christmas Day Haiku

Graham Denton

A pair of mince pies
slightly dusty, full of rum –
grandma and grandad

A Cold is Going Round

Jane Clarke

I sneeze on Leigh, he coughs on Anne,
she breathes on Yash, he holds Kim's hand,
she snuffles over Magdalena,
Raj, Yasmima, and Irina.
They sniffle and blow snotty noses
over work for Mrs Roses.
She sneezes over me and Leigh.
A cold is going round, you see.

January Poem

Catherine Benson

Flake on flake
the snow
rewrites the garden.

Word on word
the poem
settles on the page.

Snow Petrels

Liz Brownlee

On skies and seas
veiled white with light,
snow petrels weave
and wheel in flight,

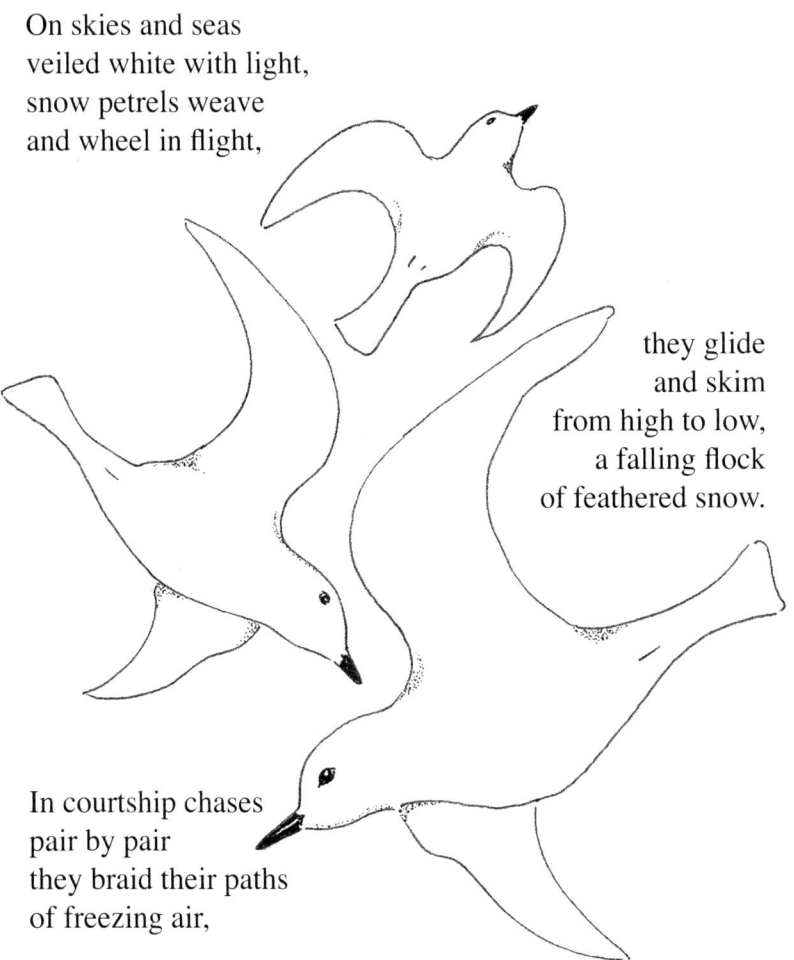

they glide
and skim
from high to low,
a falling flock
of feathered snow.

In courtship chases
pair by pair
they braid their paths
of freezing air,

birds of Antarctic
paradise;
the cliffs, the sea,
the snow, the ice.

Big Fat Budgie

Michaela Morgan

I'm a big fat budgie,
I don't do a lot.
Might park on my perch.
Might peck in my pot.
Might peek at my mirror.
Might ring my bell.
Might peer through the bars of my fat budgie cell.
Might say, "Who's a pretty boy then?"
Might not.
I'm a big fat budgie.
I don't do a lot.

Where Do the Lost Kites Go?

Jan Dean

Where do the lost kites go?
All the lost kites
When the wind comes scissoring
Across the blue
Or shears like an ice knife
Through and through?
Do they dance for long
In the wild arms of the tree?
Or become a stranger sort of gull
Above the heaving grey-humped sea?
Do they lie sad and dead upon hills
Fading hollow husks
Empty as old banana peel?
I feel the air tug and gust…
What would it be like to fly?
To just let go and rise
Forever and forever falling into skies?

The Monster from Planet Chocolate

Andrea Shavick

I'm a monster from Planet Chocolate
Chocolate ears, chocolate eyes, chocolate feet
Chocolate is all I live for
Chocolate is all I eat
Well it was…
Until I reached Planet Earth
And ate a human child
Not nearly as sweet as chocolate
And nothing like as mild
But a flavour you just can't forget
And white bony bits that go CRUNCH
I'm sending a message to the folks back home
JOIN ME ON EARTH … FOR LUNCH

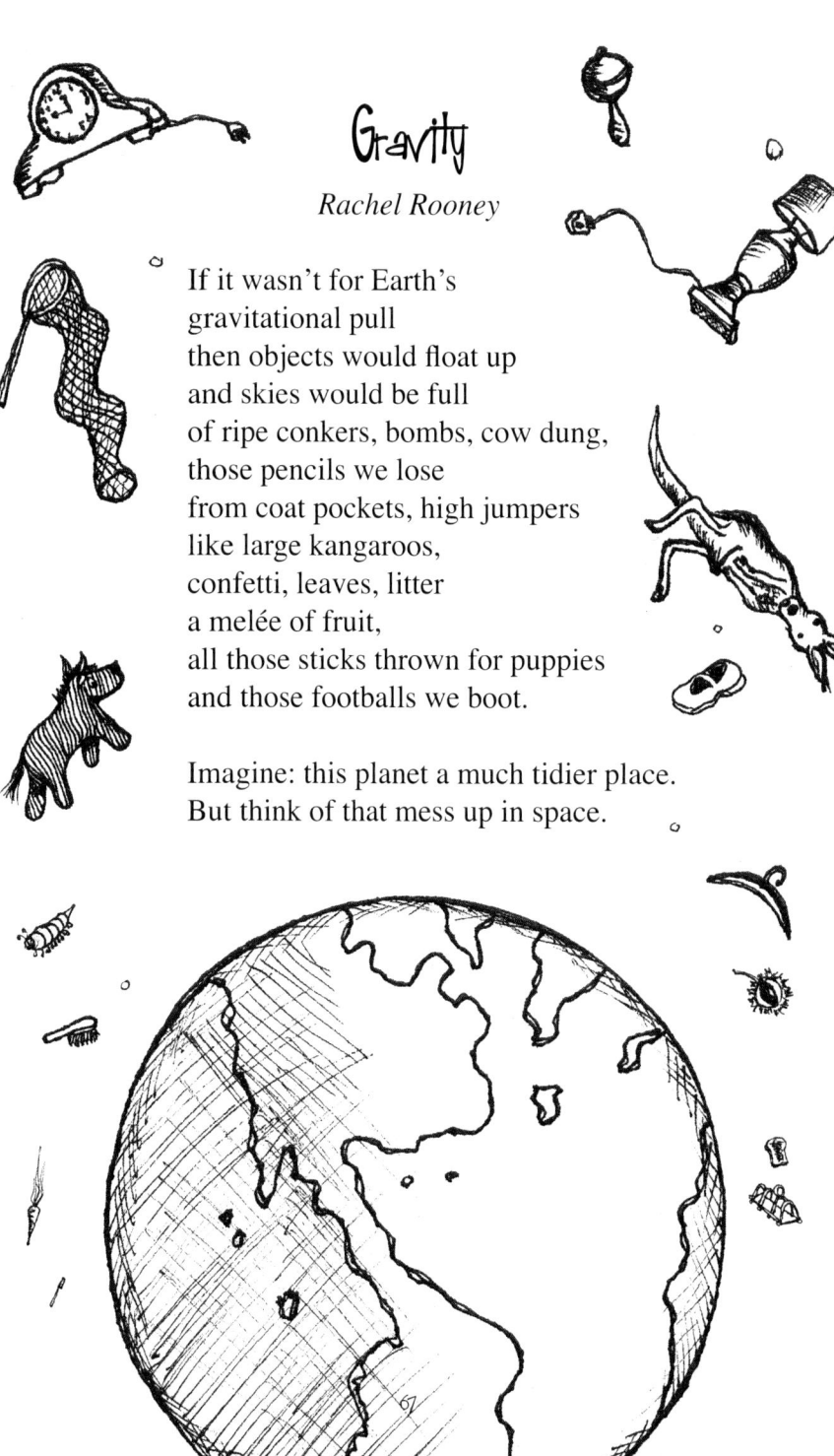

Gravity

Rachel Rooney

If it wasn't for Earth's
gravitational pull
then objects would float up
and skies would be full
of ripe conkers, bombs, cow dung,
those pencils we lose
from coat pockets, high jumpers
like large kangaroos,
confetti, leaves, litter
a melée of fruit,
all those sticks thrown for puppies
and those footballs we boot.

Imagine: this planet a much tidier place.
But think of that mess up in space.

Space Doubt

Graham Denton

When I asked my Dad
if he believed
in UFOs, or flying saucers,
or alien spacecraft
of any sort,
he just laughed.
"Don't be daft,"
was his retort.

And when I asked him
if he thought
there might be life
on other planets
like Pluto or Jupiter,
my Dad just shrugged his shoulders,
shook his head, and said,
"Pluto or Jupiter?
I think you're getting stupider!"

And when I said to my Dad,
"Dad, do you think we'll
ever get visited
by strange beings
travelling in a rocket ship?"

He said, "Now that's just plain silly.
You must think I'm a bit dippy!
To believe there's creatures from another race
somewhere deep in outer space,
I'd have to be completely mad,"
said Dad.

"Everyone knows," he said,
"the only living beings
in all of the stars
are right here
on Mars."

Boast

Rachel Rooney

I've got a friend
who swallowed a stopwatch
in three minutes and forty two and a half seconds.

I've got a friend
who swallowed a lampost.
He lives down our street.

I've got a friend
who swallowed a DVD
I've seen her do it loads of times.

I've got a friend
who swallowed a wide-screen T.V.
Now she's famous.

I've got a friend
who swallowed a fence.
He's always round our house.

I've got a friend
who swallowed a lie-detector.
Honest!

Our Baby is Howling

Jane Clarke

Our baby is howling, it just isn't right,
Winston howls and he howls all day and all night.
He howls when he's wet, he howls when he's dry,
he howls and he howls, and he doesn't know why.
He howls at our Mum and he howls at our Dad.
The howling, the howling, it's driving us mad.

At last! His first smile! It's a special day.
Is Winston changing? Will he be okay?
We're holding our breath. As we stand and stare
Winston stops howling and starts growing hair.

Hair grows on his fingers, hair grows on his toes,
hair grows on his ears and all over his nose.
Look at his teeth! Look at his nails!
Winston's so happy, he's wagging his tail.
Outside, shadows shift in the silvery gloom.
As the clouds roll away, he howls at the moon.

Yes! Winston's got it! He's got it right!
We only howl when the moon's full and bright.
Our baby's a werewolf, just like me and you.
Let's join in the howling!
A-oo-ooo, oooo-ooooo-oooooooooooooooooooo!

The Boy Who Cried Wolf

Roger Stevens

You can watch the sky
And the wind patterning the grass
And try to understand the ways of sheep
But you'll get bored
In the end
Or fall asleep.

Wolf! You cry out.
You blow your whistle, ring your bell,
Call the wolf hotline on your mobile phone
And the villagers come.
But there is no wolf.

Later, you try it again.
This time making it sound more urgent.
Come quickly. The wolf has carried off a new-born lamb!
The villagers come.
They are angry. You are sorry
But you know you'll do it again
Before the long, dreary day is through.

And where the trees meet the slopes
As the evening fades
The wolves are gathering.

My Piano. Your What? My Piano. You Haven't Got a Piano. Yes I Have.

John Rice

I have bought a piano.
It sits in the living room
on the left hand side of the window.
The sunshine falls lightly on the keys
making them gleam dully, like marzipan on a cake.
When no-one is about, I sit at the piano
and I practise playing easy tunes. Plink, plonk, plink.
I have to wait until no-one is about because
I am not very good at playing the piano. I'm learning.
I'm embarrassed if people hear my mistakes.
One day I realise it doesn't feel right
having the piano on the left hand side of the window.
So I move it to the right hand side.
The moonshine falls lightly on the keys
making them sparkle brightly, like sugar on a biscuit.
Suddenly I am playing tunes by famous composers
like Mozart and Chopin. Plinkety-tiddle, plonkety-twink.
I let people listen and I enjoy playing for them.
I haven't bought a piano. That was a lie.

(I'd like to buy a piano though)

Sounds Amazing

John Rice

The vrooommm of a jet as it lands at Gatwick,
the yaarrhhh of a striker scoring his hat-trick.

The huurrmm of a laptop as it warms up the tabletop,
the truumm of the traffic passing through Mablethorpe.

The krirp that you hear turning newspaper pages,
the grraahhh of the wild things escaping from cages.

The whaarr of the wind thrust out by propellers,
the plirps of light rain as it plops on umbrellas.

The whoogly-whoog-whoo of a common pigeon,
the purring-pray-purr as people practise religion.

The spitty-frish-glurg of a machine making coffee,
the slurp-slobber-slopp of a child chewing toffee.

The tingly-tinks of the Space Station antennae,
the swushery-swish when dancers waltz in Vienna.

Metalman

Bernard Young

I've got nerves of steel
An iron will
I'm as hard as nails
Invincible!

You can call me *Metalman*

I don't catch robbers
I don't stop crime
I get so weary
I have to take my time

OK, you can call me *Metal (fatigue) man*

You won't catch me flying
I weigh a ton
Instead of running
I lumber along

Yes, you can call me *Heavy Metalman*

I've got eyes that shine
A love that's strong
A heart of gold
A silver tongue

My girlfriend calls me *Precious*

But you'd better call me *Metalman*

THAT'S
METALMAN
TO YOU!

About That Camping Out Tonight, Dad!

Philip Waddell

Outside where it's black
As a witch's cat…
The realm of the bat
And the scuttling rat.

Outside in the haunt
Of the hooting owl…
Where foxes prowl
And spooked dogs howl.

Outside in the night
Where creatures peep,
Stalk, slither and creep…
I'd never sleep!

It's a Miss-tery

Graham Denton

I missed it on Monday,
missed it on Tuesday,
missed it on Wednesday
and Thursday, too;
on Friday, Saturday
and on Sunday—
whatever it was
I haven't a clue!

Whoo-ooo-ooo-ooooo!

Gerard Benson

Said the first ghost
On the old gate post,
"What I hate most
Is the co-o-old,
And being so o-o-old…
Five hundred years at least,
And being no use
To hen or goose,
Or man or beast.
And the wind in the trees
Which makes you freeze!"

"Whoo-ooo-ooo-ooooo!
What about you?"

Said the second ghost
On the old gate post,
"What I hate most
Is yoo-ooo-oouu,
When you suddenly say,
'Whoo-ooo-ooo-ooooo!'"

Bedtime Mysteries

Philip Waddell

Does Little Red Riding Hood
Rescue her Gran?
Is the Pied Piper
A kindly young man?
Do Hansel and Gretel
Escape from the witch?
Do Jack's magic beans
Make the simple lad rich?
Is Goldilocks eaten up
By the three bears?
Are tortoises faster
At racing than hares?
Is the old woman
In Snow White a fake?
Don't ask me, I don't know,
I can't stay awake!

Big Zeds

Sue Hardy-Dawson

It's Christmas Eve and I can't
sleep. So Mum told me, to
count
some
sheep.
But wool
is horrid
up your
nose
And one
keeps
sniffing
at my
toes.
They're
bleating,
breathing
and chewing my hair. I think
I'll just stay awake next year!

Aesop

Roger Stevens

At writing Aesop was tip top
But his limericks, alas, weren't much cop
His first lines were fine
And his rhymes were divine
But he just didn't know when to stop
And always wrote a little moral on the end.

Shouting at the Ocean

Roger Stevens

There's no point shouting at the ocean
When you're feeling low
The tide will still come in
It doesn't want to know

It's no good shouting at the ocean
Just because it's there
You can yell, throw stones or kick the sand
The ocean doesn't care

There's no use railing at the ocean
If you're angry or upset
The sea won't even notice you
It's too busy being wet

For the sea has no emotion
It doesn't hear you shout
It only listens to the moon
It just comes in and out

So if you're hurt, upset or angry
Write down all you want to say
Then post it in the ocean
Watch your troubles float away

About the Poets in this Book

Catherine Benson was a child of the seaside. When she wasn't in school she was usually on the beach, drawing and writing in the sand with a seagull's feather and collecting, collecting, collecting.

Gerard Benson, poet, actor, singer, dancer, used to be a sailor. Asked politely he'll sing you a shanty. Don't ask for a hornpipe.

Liz Brownlee has been a penguin, polar bear, panda and pufferfish because she is a poet who writes about animals. www.poetliz.co.uk

Jane Clarke's shark Gilbert the Great did not eat Andrea's grandma. He was starring in one of Jane's books at the time. www.jane-clarke.co.uk

Sue Hardy-Dawson is far too polite to shout at the ocean but has jammed with jellyfish, serenaded seaweed, dittied with dolphins and likes to write a poem or two.

Jan Dean used to spend quite a lot of time under the sea, but then she learned to swim. www.jandean.co.uk

Graham Denton is a children's poet and anthologist. Although he doesn't live anywhere near the sea, his head is always swimming with new ideas for poems and books. www.handsupbooks.co.uk

Michaela Morgan writes stories and poems for children and she lives by the grey sea in Brighton and the blue sea in France. However she never SHOUTS at the sea, she waves. www.michaelamorgan.com

John Rice is a poet and storyteller who spent his childhood exploring the beaches, rock pools and shorelines of the Scottish seaside town of Saltcoats. He now collects sea cliffs!

Rachel Rooney lives by the sea in Brighton. She's a teacher, poet and picture book writer but would rather be a mermaid.

Andrea Shavick's grandma really was eaten by a shark. This explains why she can't stop writing poems about people being gobbled up. www.shavick.com

Roger Stevens has written lots of poetry books for children. He can't swim but did manage to float once and wrote a poem about it. www.poetryzone.co.uk

Philip Waddell enjoys walking on sandy beaches and throwing sticks for Spot, his dogfish.

Bernard Young's job is writing poems and visiting schools. He can't remember ever shouting at the ocean (but he does sometimes whisper to the trees).